Beverley Sutherland S.

MALAYSIAN
& *Thai Cuisine*

The Five Mile Press

Metric/Imperial Measurements

In this book, quantities are expressed in metric
measures, with imperial equivalents in brackets.
These conversions are approximate.
The difference between exact and approximate
conversions amounts to only a teaspoon
or two, and will not affect cooking results.
A metric cup is used throughout this book.

The Five Mile Press

The Five Mile Press Pty Ltd
22 Summit Road
Noble Park Vic 3174
Australia

First published 1998

Editor: Sonya Plowman
Production: Emma Borghesi
Photography and Styling: Neil Lorimer
Cover design: Emma Borghesi
Design: Jo Waite Design

Printed in Hong Kong by Toppan.

National Library of Australia Cataloguing-in-Publication data

Sutherland Smith, Beverley.
Malaysian & Thai cuisine.

ISBN 1 86463 052 3.
1. Cookery, Thai. 2. Cookery, Malaysian. I. Title.
641.59593

Contents

Entrees and Accompaniments

Snack foods are especially popular in Asia and can be served as a first course or as a casual lunch with a bowl of rice.

Asian kitchens are very simple. Until recent times most ingredients were pounded, minced or ground by hand in ways that most of us would deem far too labour-intensive. With modern Western kitchens and appliances it is easy to make these dishes quickly, without taking away any of the intense flavours.

The recipes taste wonderful in themselves, but can also be used as a guideline for adapting to suit your own personal taste, in the same creative way that Malay and Thai people have cooked for generations.

With many of these dishes, instead of making an entire Thai or Malay meal, you may wish to incorporate them into a Western meal. The spring rolls can be eaten as a snack before a barbecue, and the crispy potato cakes can be nibbled before dinner and dipped in a sauce. The vegetable dishes and the sauces can also be served as part of a regular meal if desired.

Easy Thai Noodles
Thai

A simple noodle dish which can be served plain or garnished with spring onion, chopped roasted peanuts, coriander sprigs, garlic, chives, prawns or pieces of cooked, hot chicken. Serves 4.

. . . .

300 g dried rice stick noodles
3 tablespoons fish sauce
2 teaspoons brown sugar
2 tablespoons lemon juice

1 tablespoon sweet Thai chilli sauce
6 cloves garlic, finely chopped
185 g beanshoots

Method
Soak the noodles in hot water for 15 minutes or cook until tender. Drain. Mix in the fish sauce, with sugar, lemon juice and chilli sauce. Heat oil in a large frying pan. Fry the garlic in the oil for 30 seconds, add the sauce and noodles, and toss for a minute. Add beanshoots and cook, tossing until everything is hot. Serve immediately as these noodles break easily and become sticky if left.

Spring Rolls
Thai

These small spring rolls make ideal fingerfoods and can be served as a first course with lettuce, Asian mint and sweet Thai chilli dipping sauce. Won-ton wrappers can be bought from Asian stores. This recipe makes approximately 36 small spring rolls.

. . . .

1 cup chopped fine rice noodles,
*   soaked in warm water until soft*
3 tablespoons oil
4 cloves garlic, finely chopped
2 chillies, finely chopped
1 teaspoon ginger, finely chopped
250 g pork, finely minced
1 tablespoon fish sauce
2 teaspoons lemon juice
2 teaspoons brown sugar

1 teaspoon black pepper
1 teaspoon cornflour
125 g cooked prawns (or shrimp),
*   very finely sliced*
2 tablespoons Asian mint (or coriander),
finely chopped
36 small won-ton wrappers
2 tablespoons cornflour, mixed with
*   water to make a thin paste*

Method
Drain noodles well. Heat oil in a large frying pan and fry the garlic, chillies and ginger for a minute. Add pork and fry until well browned. Add fish sauce lemon juice, sugar and pepper. Mix cornflour with a tablespoon of water, add and stir until thickened. Add prawns and mint, and transfer to a bowl to cool. Brush wrappers lightly with water, working with 6 to 8 at a time. Put a spoonful of the filling on a point of the roll and fold over, then turn the sides in to completely enclose. Continue to roll away until there is only a little section of the point left. Brush with cornflour mix and fold it over the roll, pressing down gently but firmly. They can be left at this stage for 6 hours or frozen. To cook, heat oil to about 190°C and fry the rolls, turning over until golden brown and crisp. Drain.

Rice with Coconut Milk
Thai

This can be served instead of boiled or steamed rice for a richer flavour and subtle, slightly sweet tasting rice. Do not serve it, however, with another coconut-based main dish.

. . . .

2 cups coconut milk
1 cup water
1 teaspoon salt

1 teaspoon sugar
2 cups jasmine rice

Method
Heat the coconut milk with water, salt and sugar in a heavy based pan. When it has come to a boil, add the rice to the saucepan. Bring to a boil again, stirring. Cover and cook over a very low heat for 20 minutes. Pull the pan from the heat but don't take the lid off the saucepan for 10 minutes. It should be perfectly cooked with separate grains of rice in a slightly sticky mixture. Fluff with a couple of forks.

Beanshoots and Egg Shreds
Malaysian

With rice this makes a tasty light lunch, or can be used as a course to accompany some simple grilled chicken. The firm egg strips and the beanshoots combine well in this spicy sauce. Serves 3 with rice as a light lunch, 6 as an accompaniment.

. . . .

3 tablespoons oil
3 eggs, beaten
salt and pepper
2 cloves garlic, finely chopped

2 spring onions, cut into thin slices
1 chilli, finely chopped and seeds discarded
375 g (12 oz) beanshoots

Method
Heat a little of the oil in a frying pan. Mix the eggs with salt and pepper and pour sufficient into the pan to cover the base. Leave to set, then lift the edges and flip carefully over to cook the other side. Remove to a plate and repeat until all the egg has been used. Approximately 3 thin omelettes can be made in a 20 cm frying pan. Cool and then roll up and cut into shreds.

Add a little more oil to the pan and fry the garlic, spring onions and chilli until aromatic. Rinse the beanshoots. Add to the pan and toss until wilted. Season with salt and pepper and in the last 30 seconds of cooking add the egg shreds and carefully stir through. If desired some egg shreds may be retained to garnish the dish.

Cabbage Braised in Coconut Milk
Malaysian

Sweet, yet fresh tasting, cabbage becomes an interesting vegetable cooked in this manner. It is not out of place in a Western meal, can be served with rice as a light vegetarian dish, and is also good with roasted chicken.

. . . .

1 small onion, finely chopped
2 cloves garlic, finely chopped
1 chilli, finely chopped and seeds discarded
½ teaspoon turmeric
2 tablespoons oil
1 cup coconut milk

½ cup water
1 teaspoon salt
1 teaspoon brown sugar
¼ large or ½ small cabbage, finely shredded
2 teaspoons lemon juice

Method

Mix the onion with garlic, chilli and turmeric. Heat the oil in a large pot and fry the spices until aromatic. Pour in the coconut milk with water, season with salt and brown sugar, and bring to a boil. Add the cabbage and stir. Cook uncovered, turning over frequently until the cabbage is soft. If mixture is too thin, boil over a high heat for a few minutes. Before serving add the lemon juice.

Sauteed Mixed Greens
Thai

A fresh tasting Thai vegetable dish which can be made with any mixed variety of greens. Use as an accompaniment or with rice as a light meal. Serves 4.

. . . .

3 tablespoons oil
4 cloves garlic, finely chopped
2 shallots, finely chopped
1 chilli, finely chopped and seeds discarded
2 cups shredded lettuce

1 bunch baby bok choy cut across into thick slices
250 g (8 oz) baby spinach leaves
1 tablespoon fish sauce
2 teaspoons sugar
1 tablespoon lemon juice

Method

Heat the oil and fry the garlic, shallots and chilli until aromatic. Add the lettuce, bok choy, spinach and 1 tablespoon water and toss until the greens have wilted. Mix the fish sauce with sugar and lemon juice and add. Stir until it comes back to a boil, and toss until the greens are tender.

Rose Petal Salad
Thai

Flower petals are an important ingredient in Thai cuisine and this romantically named salad is actually quite substantial with a mix of pork, prawn and chicken. Do not use rose petals from the florist as they may be sprayed with chemicals. Serves 8 as a first course, or 4 as a main course.

. . . .

3 tablespoons oil
3 cloves chopped garlic
250 g (8 oz) finely minced pork
250 g (8 oz) cooked chicken, cut into tiny pieces
500 g (1 lb) shelled cooked prawns, cut into slices
4 tablespoons shallots, finely sliced
3 tablespoons fish sauce

1 tablespoon brown sugar
⅓ cup lemon juice
1 tablespoon sweet chilli sauce
a handful of rose petals
8 large lettuce leaves
½ cup coriander sprigs

Method

Heat half the oil and fry the garlic until a pale gold. Add the pork and keep stirring until it is broken into small pieces and quite brown. Cover the pan and cook for 5 minutes. Transfer to a bowl. Add the chicken and prawn.

Heat the remaining oil. Fry the shallots until golden and slightly crisp. Drain. Mix the fish sauce, brown sugar, lemon juice, chilli sauce and half the browned shallots. Pour over the mixture in a bowl. Toss.

Carefully fold in three quarters of the rose petals. Arrange lettuce over the base of a plate, overlapping the leaves slightly. Be sure to remove any of the hard core. Mound the meat on top. Scatter with coriander, the remaining shallots and the rest of the rose petals.

Frying the pork and garlic

Folding in the petals

Crispy Potato Cakes
Malaysian

Soft and creamy in the centre, these potato cakes have a lovely crisp outside when they are cooked. Use an old variety of potato for the nicest texture. Makes approximately 18 potato cakes.

. . . .

500 g (1 lb) potatoes
1 teaspoon salt
2 tablespoons oil
¼ cup shallots, finely chopped
2 cloves garlic, finely chopped

dash of cayenne pepper
2 tablespoons spring onion, finely chopped
2 eggs beaten with a teaspoon water
oil for deep frying

Method

Cook the potatoes in lightly salted water until tender. While they are cooking, heat the oil and fry the shallots and garlic until golden brown.   Add the cayenne and spring onion. Mash the cooked potatoes using a fork or potato masher - it does not matter if the mash is not quite smooth. Do not use a food processor as it will cause the potatoes to become gluey and tough. Mix in the spring onion and chill the potato mixture for about 6 hours.

Form into small round balls about the size of a large walnut and flatten slightly. Place beaten egg in a shallow bowl. Heat enough oil to fry the potatoes, using enough to just cover them. Dip the potatoes into the beaten egg. Shake away the excess and then slide them carefully into the oil. Cook for about 2 minutes or until crisp and brown.

Spicy Satay Sauce
Malaysian

This sauce is served with chicken and other meats and adds a wonderful nutty flavour to all dishes.

. . . .

2 cloves chopped garlic
3 tablespoons finely chopped onion
3 tablespoons oil
¾ cup peanuts
2 tablespoons soy sauce

2 teaspoons brown sugar
1 cup coconut milk
½ cup water
1 tablespoon lemon juice
1 chilli, finely chopped

Method

Heat the garlic and onion in the oil for a few minutes. Add the peanuts and cook gently until coloured. Remove and put into a food processor with the soy sauce, brown sugar and half the coconut milk. When the mixture has turned into a paste transfer to a saucepan and add the remainder of the coconut milk, water, lemon juice and chilli. Simmer gently for 10 minutes or until thickened. Remove. Can be stored in a covered jar in the refrigerator for about 5 days and warmed again before serving.

Green Curry Paste

Thai

This aromatic spicy paste is the base for Thai green curry dishes and the advantage of making it at home is that the heat can be varied according to personal taste. It can be stored for 2 to 3 weeks in the refrigerator or frozen for 2 months. As a rule green chillies are in season in late summer, autumn and early winter. The green colour comes not from the chilli but the coriander added at the finish.

Take care when handling big quantities of chilli. It is a good idea to wear fine rubber gloves when cutting them up, then to rinse the gloves while they are still on your hands to wash away the chilli oil.

. . . .

2 tablespoons green fresh chillies (serrano)
4 hot green chillies (New Mexico or Anaheim), seeds discarded
3 stalks lemon grass
1 large onion, very finely chopped
6 cloves garlic, finely chopped
1 tablespoon grated fresh ginger

3 tablespoons chopped coriander roots and stems
¼ teaspoon ground cloves
2 teaspoons ground coriander
2 teaspoons grated lemon rind
1 tablespoon fish sauce
½ cup chopped coriander leaves

Method

Cut the chillies into halves and chop finely. Cut away the long ends of the lemon grass, leaving just the thick stalk end of about 10 cm. Remove the outer tough part and chop the lemon grass up finely. Blend in a food processor or blender with all the ingredients except the coriander leaves and process to a medium fine paste.

Sprinkle the coriander leaves on the sauce to produce a green speckled appearance. Pour into a sterilised jar and seal with a lid.

Main courses

Rice is an integral part of everyday life in most Asian countries, with the huge family rice cooker and bowls of rice always present on the table. To make a complete meal most of the recipes in this section should be served with rice.

Malay cuisine can be very spicy and is a result of centuries of outside influences. Meals can thus be quite diverse in nature, using a range of different ingredients. As in Thai cuisine, generous amounts of coconut milk is used to make rich, delicious sauces, and spices such as tamarind give fresh, sharp flavours to many dishes.

In Thailand an ideal meal consists of a mixture of sweet, sour, bitter, salty and spicy foods. This is generally not difficult as many dishes combine all these elements. Rice is an all-important staple to be served with each meal as it balances the spiciness of the other foods.

Spices for both Malay and Thai cuisine are easy to find in any good Asian store and are sometimes also available in supermarkets. When grinding spices, put them into a blender or processor when they are dry. This way if they are too coarse you can add a little water or oil to assist them in becoming a paste. A pestle and mortar is an excellent addition for grinding spices, though it is a little more time consuming.

The selection of dishes I have chosen have common ingredients and are simple to cook. Many of these meals can often be prepared in advance - you can chop the meats and vegetables and grind the spices when convenient and finish off the dish later. Curry dishes and soups reheat very well.

Nonya Chicken with Soy Lemon Sauce
Malaysian

This easy nonya dish is distinguished by a deeply coloured brown sauce with a spicy lemon flavour. Use thigh or drumsticks with the bone in for added sweetness and to keep the chicken succulent. Serves 4 with rice as an accompaniment.

. . . .

8 chicken drumsticks or thigh portions
3 tablespoons oil
2 onions, halved then sliced very thinly
1 chilli, cut into fine shreds and seeds removed

1 tablespoon brown sugar
2 tablespoons soy sauce
½ cup chicken stock
1 tablespoon lemon juice

Method

Pat the chicken dry. Heat half the oil in a wok or wide saucepan and add the onions and chilli. Fry, stirring for about 5 minutes until the onions have wilted, then turn up the heat and cook until they have specks of gold. Remove. Add the remaining oil and brown the chicken on all sides. Return the onions to the saucepan and mix through.

Mix the sugar, soy sauce and chicken stock and pour over the top. Cover and cook over low heat for 10 minutes. Remove the lid. Continue cooking, turning the chicken over every so often until it is cooked through and there is just a little dark, rich sauce around each portion. Squeeze lemon juice on top and shake or stir through. Serve immediately.

Chicken and Eggplant Curry
Thai

Thai eggplants are small, stubby, and roundish, and are quite different to the usual Mediterranean eggplant. If unable to find these, plain eggplants or the long Japanese ones can be substituted, but peel some strips of the skin away and cut the eggplant into large cubes. Alternatively the dish can be made using a cup of fresh baby peas. Serves 3 to 4 people when served with rice.

. . . .

500 g (1 lb) boned, skinned chicken thighs
   or drumsticks
1 tablespoon oil
1 tablespoon spicy canned curry paste or up to
   ⅓ cup green curry paste
1½ cups coconut milk
⅓ cup water

250 g (8 oz) eggplant
2 teaspoons brown sugar
1 tablespoon fish sauce
4 fresh Kaffir lime leaves, the centre vein of
   each one removed
¼ cup small whole basil leaves

Method

Cut each chicken portion into halves or three pieces. Heat the oil and fry the curry paste for a minute, add half the coconut milk and bring to a boil. Cook, stirring until there is a light film of oil on the top. Add the remaining coconut milk and bring to a boil. Add the chicken pieces, submerging them, cover and cook for about 5 minutes or until almost cooked through. Add the water, eggplant, brown sugar, fish sauce and lime leaves. Continue cooking uncovered for a further 8 minutes or until the eggplant is quite tender. Stir occasionally and if using large eggplants, cover the pan to tenderise. Lastly add the basil leaves and heat through for one minute.

Chicken Satay
Malaysian

Satay, whether Thai or Malaysian, is recognised all over the world as one of the most flavoursome of all kebab dishes. Pork and beef are also suitable meats for a satay, but use lean, cubed meat for even cooking. Makes 12 satay sticks.

. . . .

4 boned, skinned chicken breasts
2 cloves garlic, roughly chopped
8 coriander roots
2 tablespoons shallots, roughly chopped
good pinch chilli powder
1 teaspoon salt

1 teaspoon sugar
½ teaspoon coriander
½ teaspoon turmeric
2 tablespoons oil
1 tablespoon white vinegar
4 tablespoons coconut milk

Method

Put the chicken between some plastic wrap and pound gently until it is an even thickness. Cut into small cubes or long strips. Blend garlic, coriander roots, shallots, chilli powder, salt, sugar, coriander and turmeric in a processor or blender until a coarse paste. Add oil, vinegar and half the coconut milk and process again. Add the chicken to the mix, stir until coated, cover and refrigerate for 12 hours.

Soak some bamboo skewers in water for 1 hour then thread the chicken on to the skewers. Preheat the griller. Brush the skewers with the remaining coconut milk. Grill for about 3 minutes until cooked on one side, turning them over and then cooking on the other side. Brush several times with coconut milk if chicken begins to dry out.

Serve with some Spicy Satay Sauce.

Cutting chicken into strips

Threading chicken on skewers

Grilled Beef Salad
Thai

A main course or first course salad which is quite simple to make with roasted or barbecued rare beef layered on lettuce and noodles. The secret is the sauce - spicy, fresh and fragrant, it coats the beef, noodles and lettuce to create a lovely light dish. This is best served soon after it is made at room temperature. Makes 4 main course servings, 6 to 8 first course servings.

. . . .

Beef and noodles
600 g (1⅕ lb) fillet or rump steak
some black pepper
1 chilli, finely chopped and seeds discarded
1 teaspoon salt
1 tablespoon finely chopped lemon grass
250 g (8 oz) fine noodles, such as vermicelli
about 6 to 8 lettuce leaves
8 shredded mint leaves
8 coriander sprigs
10 basil leaves, cut into shreds
1 small red onion, cut into wafer thin rings

Dressing
4 cloves garlic, finely chopped
1 chilli, sliced and seeds removed
3 tablespoons fish sauce
3 tablespoons brown sugar
6 tablespoons lemon juice
3 tablespoons water

Garnish
small basil leaves
¼ cup roughly chopped dry roasted peanuts
a little extra chilli shreds (optional)

To cook the beef and noodles
Pat the beef dry. Mix the pepper with chilli, salt and lemon grass and rub into the outside of the beef. Let stand for several hours. Either roast, grill or saute until browned on the outside but be sure it is quite rare in the centre. Remove and wrap, and leave to cool completely. This can be done up to 8 hours in advance. When cool, slice wafer thin.

Cook the noodles until tender, drain and rinse. Put the lettuce on a platter. Scatter with the mint, coriander and basil. Mix noodles with a few tablespoons of dressing. Put noodles on the lettuce and then arrange beef on top, decorating beef with onion.

The dressing
Put all the ingredients into a food processor until well blended. Alternatively, crush the garlic, put into a bowl and mix everything else into this. Pour over the top of the dish. Scatter with basil, nuts and if you wish, more chilli.

Beef Curry
Thai

There are many versions of Thai curry dishes made with beef. They can be made very hot and spicy, or slightly milder and a little sweeter in cities such as Bangkok. The method given here is the traditional one. Chicken can be substituted if desired. If lime leaves aren't available, the equivalent quantity of baby lemon leaves can be used instead. Serves 4 with rice.

. . . .

Spice base
2 dried chillies, soaked for 1 hour in hot
  water and drained
2 tablespoons finely chopped lemon grass
2 tablespoons finely chopped shallots
5 cloves garlic, finely chopped
1 teaspoon salt
1 tablespoon finely chopped ginger or galangal
2 tablespoons water
1 teaspoon shrimp paste

Curry
1 cup coconut milk
600 g (1¹/₅ lb) trimmed, grilling quality beef, cut
  into thin strips about 5 cm long
¹/₄ cup water
1 tablespoon fish sauce
4 Kaffir lime leaves, centre vein removed and
  finely shredded
1 tablespoon brown sugar
20 basil leaves
¹/₂ cup dry roasted peanuts, processed to
  make a paste
some additional shreds of chilli for garnish if desired
some additional basil leaves

To make the spice base

Process all the spice base ingredients until finely ground. Remove. This can be stored refrigerated for up to a week.

To make the curry

Pour half the coconut milk into a heavy based saucepan and add the spice base. Cook for 3 minutes, stirring until aromatic and the coconut milk has thickened. Add the remaining coconut milk and bring back to a boil. Add the beef and water and simmer very gently for a couple of minutes. Mix in the fish sauce, lime leaves, sugar, basil leaves and stir for 3 minutes. Add the nuts and mix through. Serve with shreds of chilli and basil leaves on top.

Fried Rice
Malaysian

This style of fried rice is a great favourite, and makes a substantial meal served with lettuce, cucumber and tomato, with a fried egg on top and some prawn crackers alongside. Cook the rice the day beforehand and spread it out onto a flat tray overnight. It will be quite firm, with the rice grains remaining separate and absorbing the flavours without becoming soft during cooking. Serves 4.

. . . .

4 cups cold cooked long grain rice

3 chillies, finely chopped and seeds discarded

6 cloves garlic, finely chopped

1/3 cup warm water

4 tablespoons oil

250 g (8 oz) shrimp or prawns cut into thick slices

1/4 cup chopped shallots or brown onion

125 g (4 oz) chopped beans, cooked for 5 minutes

4 spring onions, cut into thin slices

salt and pepper

4 tablespoons sweet soy sauce

4 lettuce leaves

2 tomatoes, cut into thin slices

1/2 cucumber, peeled, scored and cut wafer thin

4 eggs

8 cooked prawn crackers

Method

Gently hand-rub the rice to separate the grains. Make a sauce by putting the chillies, garlic and water into a blender or small food processor. Heat 2 tablespoons of oil in a wok, add the blended sauce and cook for about 5 minutes or until a thin paste. Remove and wipe out the pan.

Cook the shrimp or prawns with shallots in remaining oil until pink, add the rice, beans, spring onions, salt and pepper, and sweet soy sauce. Toss over the heat for about 5 minutes or until very hot. Put aside and keep warm. Put lettuce on a plate, then tomato and cucumber. Fry the eggs in a little oil at the last minute, until soft in the centre. Pile the rice onto 4 plates, place an egg on top of each pile and place prawn crackers on the side.

Spicy Patties
Thai

These look exactly like hamburger patties but taste much more exciting. Serve with some salad and rice or noodles for a simple, yet great easy meal. The beef can be substituted with pork to make an all-pork dish if preferred. Makes 8 patties.

. . . .

4 cloves garlic, finely chopped
1 tablespoon coriander root, chopped
1 teaspoon ground black pepper
¼ cup coriander leaves
1 small onion, finely chopped
250 g (8 oz) finely minced lean pork
250 g (8 oz) finely minced beef

1 tablespoon fish sauce
1 tablespoon cold water
2 teaspoons brown sugar
1 egg
1 tablespoon lemon juice
oil to cook the patties

Method

Mix the garlic, coriander root, black pepper and coriander leaves in a bowl and mash them together very well. Put into a basin. Add onion, pork, beef, fish sauce, water, sugar, and egg combined with lemon juice. Using your hands, mix in a circular fashion until the meat binds well. Chill covered for an hour and then form into round patties about the size of a coffee saucer. These can be kept covered in the refrigerator for about 8 hours.

Heat a little oil in a frying pan and saute the patties on both sides until cooked through. Drain on some kitchen paper and serve.

Mixing the ingredients

Forming the patties

Laksa

Malaysian

A rich and substantial combination of soup and stew with a fragrant spicy liquid around a mix of noodles, chicken and prawns, Laksa is usually eaten as a main course. As it takes some time to prepare, it can be divided into stages. You can prepare the sauce and mix the spices during the day, then cook the dish when ready. To save time you can buy Laksa spice base ready mixed in Asian shops and some good delicatessens. The recipe is started off this way by simply cooking the spices over a low heat.

Coriander can be used as a substitute for Vietnamese mint, though a different flavour will be imparted to the dish. The Malay name for Vietnamese mint is "Daun Kesum" and is much more pungent and quite differently flavoured to plain mint.

. . . .

Spices

¹/₂ teaspoon turmeric
¹/₂ teaspoon shrimp paste
4 chillies, chopped and seeds discarded
4 shallots, roughly chopped
1 stalk lemon grass, cut into small pieces
2 tablespoons shreds of galangal or ginger

Sauce

6 tablespoons oil
2 sprigs Vietnamese mint or 'Laksa leaf'
6 cups water
1¹/₂ cups coconut milk
1 tablespoon brown sugar
¹/₂ teaspoon salt

To finish the dish

3 eggs
1 skinned chicken breast, cut into fine shreds
12 green prawns, shelled
375 g (12 oz) fresh yellow noodles or cooked fine dried noodles
3 spring onions, finely sliced
some additional Vietnamese mint or coriander

To make the sauce

Grind all the spice ingredients. Add 2 tablespoons of oil and grind again. Heat the remaining oil and cook the spices over a low heat, stirring for about 5 minutes or until very fragrant. Add the Vietnamese mint and water and bring back to a boil. Stir in the coconut milk with sugar and salt. Simmer over low heat for 10 minutes. While this is cooking beat the eggs. Brush a 20 cm pan with oil and make 2 omelettes with the eggs. Roll up and slice thinly. This can be done well in advance up to this stage.

To finish the dish

Reheat the sauce. Add the chicken and prawn. Put a lid on top and cook gently for about 3 minutes. Put the noodles into a large bowl. Pour boiling water over them to separate and heat them again.

Add equal amounts of noodles to 4 large deep soup bowls. Ladle the sauce over the noodles, dividing the prawns so each person has 4. Scatter on some spring onion, omelette strips and more Vietnamese mint or coriander. Serve with some wedges of lime or lemon on the table and a bowl of thinly sliced red chilli for those who like it very hot.

Pork Soup with Noodles
Thai

This particular soup uses roast pork and the easiest way is to buy some Chinese roasted pork and then slice it very finely. Alternatively, buy a pork fillet and cook it yourself at home, marinating it first in a clove of crushed garlic, 1 teaspoon fresh ginger, 1 tablespoon fish sauce, 2 teaspoons brown sugar and 1 tablespoon lemon juice for 12 hours. Then bake in the oven on a rack with a tray underneath which has a little water for between 25 and 45 minutes, depending on its thickness, until tender. Serves 4.

. . . .

2 tablespoons oil
4 cloves garlic, finely sliced
5 cups well flavoured chicken stock
4 finely shredded lettuce leaves
150 g (5 oz) rice vermicelli or egg noodle
150 g (5 oz) bean shoots
1 tablespoon fish sauce

1 tablespoons brown sugar
285 g (9½ oz) cooked roast pork, cut into very thin slices
1 chilli, finely chopped and seeds discarded
4 spring onions, finely chopped, including some green
2 tablespoons chopped coriander sprigs
2 tablespoons roughly chopped dry roasted peanuts

Method
Heat the oil and fry the garlic until a pale gold. Drain on kitchen paper. Heat the stock and when boiling add the lettuce. Cook for about 3 minutes, then add the noodles and cook 3 or more minutes or until tender. Add the beanshoots, fried garlic, fish sauce, sugar, pork and chilli. Bring back to a boil. Spoon immediately into soup bowls and scatter with spring onion, coriander and peanuts.

Nonya Pork in Coconut Milk
Malaysian

This Nonya dish is a combination of Chinese and Malaysian influences. The Malaysian spices and coconut milk produce a rich, nutty flavoured sauce around the pork. Chicken pieces can be used as a substitute for pork if preferred. Serves 4 with rice.

. . . .

1 large brown onion, finely chopped
2 shallots, finely chopped
2 chillies, finely chopped and seeds discarded
⅓ cup macadamia nuts
½ teaspoon dried shrimp paste
1 clove garlic, finely chopped
1 tablespoon oil

500 g (1 lb) pork fillets, cut into bite sized pieces
¾ cup water
½ teaspoon salt
1 cup coconut cream
1 tablespoon brown sugar
3 tablespoons lemon juice

Method
Put the onion, shallots, chillies, nuts, shrimp paste and garlic into a blender or food processor until a coarse paste. Heat oil in a heavy based pan and cook the paste for a few minutes until aromatic. Add the pork and stir until well coated with spices. When the pork has changed colour add the water, season with salt and cover. Cook gently for 20 minutes. Mix in the coconut cream and sugar and continue cooking until a thick sauce has formed. Squeeze in the lemon juice and stir through. Serve immediately.

Fragrant Lamb Meatballs

Malaysian

These interesting little meatballs go well on top of a dish of fried rice, with some noodles, or just alongside a salad. A relish such as a chutney or some spicy chilli sauce can be used as an accompaniment. Ask the butcher to mince lamb from the shoulder, neck or leg for this dish. Fresh oil may be required for each batch. For an untraditional variation, this mixture can be formed into hamburger patties and cooked in a frying pan. Makes approximately 24 meatballs.

. . . .

500 g (1 lb) finely minced lamb
2 cloves garlic, finely chopped
¼ cup finely chopped fresh coriander
1 small onion, finely chopped
½ teaspoon turmeric
¼ teaspoon ground cumin
1 teaspoon ground coriander

1 teaspoon salt
1 teaspoon black pepper
¼ teaspoon cayenne pepper
1 egg
1 tablespoon plain flour
oil to cook the meatballs

Method

Put the lamb and everything but the egg and flour in the bowl and stir through. Add egg and scatter flour on top. Mix very well with hands until thoroughly blended. With wet hands take out tablespoon sizes of the mixture and form into meatballs. They can be refrigerated at this stage for 8 hours.

Pour sufficient oil into a shallow saucepan to cover a depth of about 1.5 cm. When hot add the meatballs a few at a time. If the oil is cool, they will stick to the pan. Cook for about 3 minutes or until well coloured, turning them over carefully while frying. As they are browned and cooked remove to the oven to keep warm while the rest are frying.

Drain on some kitchen paper and serve immediately.

Lamb Curry
Malaysian

In Malaysia this dish is made with older sheep, but sweet young lamb is suggested here as it gives a better flavour. As the curry contains potatoes there is no need to serve with rice. Serves 4.

. . . .

1 tablespoon tamarind pulp
¼ cup hot water
2 teaspoons ground cumin
½ teaspoon ground fennel
2 teaspoons ground coriander
½ teaspoon black peppercorns
½ teaspoon turmeric
¼ teaspoon ground nutmeg
1 brown onion, finely chopped
3 cloves garlic, finely chopped

1 tablespoon chopped fresh ginger
2 chillies, finely chopped and seeds discarded
1 tablespoon oil
750 g (1½ lb) lamb, cut from the shoulder or leg, cubes about 5 cm square
2 cups water
1 teaspoon salt
1 cinnamon stick
500 g (10 oz) small waxy potatoes, cut into halves
1 cup coconut milk

Method

Soak the tamarind in hot water and leave for 20 minutes. Squeeze the pulp and strain. Discard the pulp and retain the liquid. Mix the cumin, fennel and coriander together with peppercorns, turmeric and nutmeg. Grind the onion, garlic, ginger and chillies in a blender or food processor until a coarse paste.

Heat the oil in a heavy based saucepan. Add the onion mixture and cook 2 minutes, then add the mixed spices and cook a further 3 minutes, stirring continually. Add the meat and stir until it is well coated with spices. Pour in water, season with salt, add cinnamon stick and cover the pan. Cook about 20 minutes over low heat, add the potatoes and cook until the meat and potatoes are tender. Add the coconut milk and tamarind liquid. Cook uncovered a further 20 minutes, stirring gently every so often until the sauce has thickened.

Note: If you wish to reduce the sauce, strain and boil rapidly.

Hot and Sour Prawn Soup
Thai

Dom Yam Gung is one of the most popular and famous of all the fish Thai soups. Fresh with lemon grass, it is a rich spicy broth, with tender prawns floating in lime juice. The base is chicken stock, not fish stock as you may imagine, and it is important that the stock is clear and well flavoured. Equal amounts of lemon can be used instead of lime if preferred. This makes 4 generous servings.

. . . .

500 g (1 lb) fresh prawns in the shell
2 tablespoons oil
4 cups chicken stock
2 stalks lemon grass, roughly smashed with a knife
5 lime leaves
1 teaspoon lime shreds
piece 2.5 cm long fresh galangal (or fresh ginger)

1 chilli, cut into strips, seeds discarded
1 tablespoon fish sauce
2 teaspoons sugar
2 tablespoons lime or lemon juice
salt to taste
3 spring onions, finely chopped
3 tablespoons coriander sprigs, coarsely chopped

Method
Peel the prawns, rinse the shells and dry on kitchen paper. Heat the oil in a saucepan, add the prawn shells and stir until they are pink. Pour the stock over the top, add lemon grass, lime leaves, lime shreds, galangal, chilli and bring to a boil. Cover and cook over low heat for 20 minutes. Pour through a strainer and return to a clean saucepan. This part of the dish can be made hours in advance. Bring back to a boil. Add the prawns and leave over a low heat for 2 to 3 minutes, depending on their size.

Mix in fish sauce, sugar, lime juice and add salt to taste. Pour into soup bowls, dividing up the prawns equally between each bowl. Scatter the top of each one with spring onion and coriander sprigs. For those who enjoy really hot food, a few more fine shreds of fresh chilli can be added.

Spicy Fish Cakes
Thai

Fish is used in all manner of clever ways in Thailand. These spicy cakes can be made with any style of fish except those with fine flesh such as whiting. Often sold in gourmet take-away shops, these firm fish cakes are simple and much less expensive to make at home. This recipe makes about 12 small fish cakes.

. . . .

*500 g (1 lb) boned, skinned fish, cut into
  2 .5 cm pieces*
½ teaspoon salt
1 tablespoon grated fresh ginger
2 cloves chopped garlic
1 chilli, chopped and seeds discarded

1 tablespoon lemon grass, very finely chopped
2 tablespoons spring onions, chopped small
1 tablespoon fish sauce
1 teaspoon sugar
a little oil to cook the cakes

Method

Put the fish and salt into a food processor until finely chopped. Add the ginger, garlic, chilli, lemon grass, spring onions, fish sauce and sugar and process again until well blended. Don't mix too long as it will turn into a sticky paste. Remove to a bowl. With wet hands take out heaped tablespoon-sized balls of the mixture and flatten to about 1 cm in size. Chill for up to 6 hours.

Heat some oil in a frying pan. Add the fish cakes and cook until a golden brown colour on the outside, turning half way through the cooking. Turn down the heat after a minute or two, and be sure they are cooked to the centre. Do not overcook as the flesh will become dry. Drain on kitchen paper and serve with a cucumber salad.

Chopped ingredients

Mussels with Lemon Grass and Basil
Thai

This dish features steamed mussels layered with Thai herbs to form a fragrant briny sauce. A spicy dip is served on the table which can either be spooned into the sauce or used as a dip for the mussels. Remember to put a large bowl on the table for discarded mussel shells. Serves 4 to 6.

. . . .

2 kg baby mussels
1 cup water
4 garlic cloves finely chopped
1 chilli, finely chopped and seeds discarded
3 stalks lemon grass, cut into thick slices
8 kaffir lime leaves, centre vein removed or
*   some baby lemon leaves*

½ teaspoon salt
2 teaspoons sugar
1 chilli, finely chopped and seeds discarded
¼ cup coriander sprigs
an additional 4 cloves garlic, finely chopped
2 tablespoons lemon juice

Method
Wash the mussels, scrub and remove the beard. Discard any that are open. Put the water into a large wide saucepan. Add half the garlic, chilli and lemon grass. Put mussels on top and then the remaining garlic, chilli and lemon grass. Add lime leaves. Bring to a boil. Cover and steam, shaking the pot occasionally until the mussels have opened. While they are cooking pound or process the salt, sugar, chilli, coriander and garlic until a coarse paste. Add lemon juice.

Take out the mussels and divide them between four bowls. Strain the liquid over the top. Serve with the pounded spices in a little dish on the table, and scatter some spices on top of the broth. Eat the mussels and then add the remaining pounded spices to the broth.

Spicy Prawns
Malaysian

An easy dish with a mix of sharp, fresh, hot, sweet and sour flavourings. Serves 4 with rice.

. . . .

750 g (1½ lb) peeled green prawns
1 chilli, finely chopped and seeds removed
3 cloves garlic, crushed
1 tablespoon finely chopped or grated ginger
1 teaspoon prawn paste
3 tablespoons oil

⅓ cup cashew nuts
3 large ripe peeled tomatoes
1 teaspoon salt
1 tablespoon sugar
2 tablespoons lemon juice

Method
Carefully remove the dark vein from the back of the prawn. Blend the chilli, garlic, ginger, prawn paste, oil and cashew nuts in a blender or food processor until a paste.

Heat a tablespoon of oil in a wok and add the paste. Cook for 30 seconds until aromatic. Add the prawns and fry, stirring until they are coated with spices. Turn the heat low and cook for 2 minutes, turning them over until they have changed colour. Add the tomatoes, salt, and sugar and continue cooking for 5 minutes until the tomatoes have formed a thick sauce. Lastly squeeze over the lemon juice and stir through.

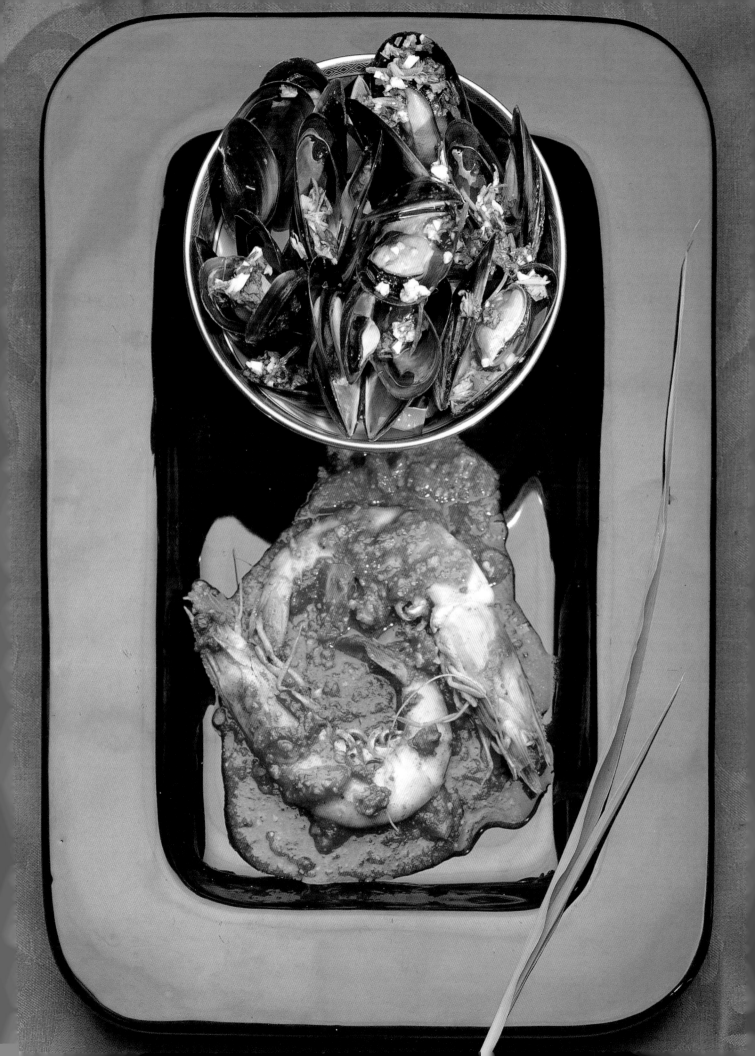

Tamarind Fish Stew
Malaysian

A slightly tart stew, served in soup bowls with a fragrant aroma, this can be made with any medium to coarse flesh fish. The original versions have as many as 10 chillies but unless cooking for those who can cope with really fiery food, 2 chillies is the recommended quantity. If fresh galangal is unavailable it can be substituted with fresh ginger, producing a similar result. Serves 4 with a bowl of rice.

. . . .

500 g (1 lb) fish, cut into thick fillets
2 stalks lemon grass, finely chopped
1 teaspoon turmeric powder
2 chillies, cut into fine shreds and seeds discarded
A 2.5 cm piece of galangal, peeled and chopped
2 tablespoons chopped shallots or brown onion
½ teaspoon dried shrimp paste

1 tablespoon tamarind pulp
3 cups warm water
2 tablespoons oil
3 teaspoons brown sugar
1 teaspoon salt
lemon juice (optional)

Method
Cut the fish into pieces about 5 cm in size.

Place the spices of lemon grass, turmeric, chilli, galangal, shallots (or brown onion) and shrimp paste into a blender or food processor until coarsely ground and well mixed. Mix the tamarind and warm water and stand for 20 minutes. Squeeze and strain out the pulp and seeds of the tamarind. Discard these and retain the liquid.

Heat the oil in a saucepan and fry the blended spice mix until aromatic. Add the tamarind liquid with sugar and salt and bring to a boil. Simmer gently for 5 minutes. Add the fish pieces and push them under the liquid. Simmer gently for about 3 to 4 minutes or until the fish is cooked through. Lemon may be added to produce a tart flavour.

Note: Galangal is a very hard root to peel and chop and caution must be taken when cutting it. Chop away from you, not towards you. Ginger may be substituted if desired.

Acknowledgements

The author and publisher express their gratitude to David Jones, Bourke Street, Melbourne, for the loan of china and table linen for use in the photographs. Gratitude is also extended to Poh Im Chua and family for providing ornaments for use in the photographs.

Index